ITALERCARS

FERRARI • LAMBORGHINI • PAGANI

Paul Mason

W
FRANKLIN WATTS
LONDON • SYDNEY

Franklin Watts
Published in Great Britain in 2018 by
The Watts Publishing Group

Copyright © The Watts Publishing
Group 2017

Executive editor: Adrian Cole
Series designer: Mayer Media
Design manager: Peter Scoulding
Picture researcher: Diana Morris

Photo acknowledgements:
Alfa Romeo Automobiles S.p.A: 24t, 24-25c,
29br. Anabela88/Shutterstock: 7b, 11b, 13b,
27b. Automobili Lamborghini S.p.A: 1t, 1b,
3t, 3b, 4-5t, 12-13, 13c. 14-15, 15t, 16t, 16-
17. Bugatti Automobiles S.A.S: 26-27, 27c.
Chameleon's Eye: 28c. Ferrari S.p.A: front
cover b, 6tl, 6-7c, 7t., 8-9c, 9t, 10tl, 10-11,
30tl, 30tr, 31t. Sergio Gutierrez Getino/
Shutterstock: 20tr. Imaenginge/Dreamstime:
5b, 29bl. Sergey Kohl/shutterstock: 4b, 30cl,
30 cr. Lancia Automobiles S.p.A: 30bl. Teddy
Leung/Shutterstock: 29c. Maserati S.p.A:
front cover t, 18bl, 18-19c, 18br. Mazzanti
Automobilii: 28b. Mr. Choppers/CC Wikimedia
Commons: 30br. Naiyyer/shutterstock: 28t.
Pagani Automobili S.p.A: 20-21, 22-23c, 23t,
32b. Betto Rodrigues/Shutterstock: 29tl.

ISBN 978 1 4451 5138 0

Printed in China

Franklin Watts
An imprint of
Hachette Children's Group
Part of The Watts Publishing Group
Carmelite House
50 Victoria Embankment
London EC4Y 0DZ

An Hachette UK Company
www.hachette.co.uk

www.franklinwatts.co.uk

MIX
Paper from
responsible sources
FSC® C104740
FSC
www.fsc.org

Contents

70000050098

WITHDRAWN FROM STOCK

Words highlighted in **bold** can be found in the glossary

Italy is where the supercar was invented, in 1966. Since then, the country has produced more supercars than any other.

THE FIRST SUPERCAR

In 1966, Lamborghini was a famous tractor manufacturer. The company owner got so tired of his Ferrari breaking down that he decided to build his own car. The result was the Miura. The Miura was so good that it invented a whole new category of car: the supercar.

The Miura is over 50 years old, so it is very different from today's supercars. Even so, many of its characteristics are shared with the most cutting-edge supercars ever built.

JUST WHAT *IS* A SUPERCAR?

There is no agreed definition of what makes a car a supercar. In Italy, though, no car would be called a supercar unless it was:

- really expensive
- made in tiny numbers
- as high-performance as possible
- very fast, and probably very light
- tricky to drive
- useless for bringing home a week's shopping, going on a camping trip, taking kids to school, etc.

The Lamborghini Miura, the world's first supercar. 764 were built between 1966 and 1973, when production ceased.

Spares: there was a spare wheel under the bonnet! (These are NOT usually found on modern supercars)

Price Tag...

When it first appeared in 1966, the Miura cost around £16,500 – equivalent to £120,000 today. Miuras are so rare though, that they have gone up in value. A lot. In 2015, one was sold for £2,000,000.

The Maserati Ghibli was launched in 1967, with sleek 'supercar' styling.

TOP SPEED

277 kph
(172 mph)

0–100 KPH

7.0 seconds

MAX POWER

262 kW
350 bhp @ 7,000 rpm

MAX **TORQUE**

369 Nm
262 lb/ft @ 5,000 rpm

Max RPM:
7,850

Engine:
3929 cc

Weight:
1,125 kg

Fuel use per 100 km (estimated):
21 litres

Gearbox:
5-speed

Drive:
rear wheels

Main body:
aluminium
(Steel doors)

Frame:
steel

Braking:
hydraulic discs

Seating: two seats – very few supercars have room for more than one passenger!

Drive: rear-wheel drive, which is harder to control but allows a faster car with more grip

Body shape: styled by famous car-design company Bertone

Engine: **mid-mounted**, shares the engine's weight between all four wheels more equally than a front-mounted engine and helps the car grip the road

Speed: the Miura was the world's fastest **production car**, able to reach almost 300 kph

The 1947 Ferrari 125 S was the start of Ferrari's supercar story.

FERRARI
488 GTB/SPIDER

When the 488 **GTB** appeared in 2015, a lot was expected of it. It replaced the 458 Italia – one of the most popular Ferraris ever made. Fortunately, the 488 GTB delivered.

Factory: Maranello, Italy

The Ferrari 458 Italia was released in 2009.

Turbo-charged engine – the first in a mid-engined Ferrari V8

'Blown spoiler' pulls air from bottom of rear screen out through rear bumper

Air scoops inspired by Ferrari 308 GTB. Upper scoop feeds turbo. Lower scoop feeds air behind car, increasing grip.

Ferrari skilfully blended new shapes with ideas from famous older Ferraris. The 488's side air scoops, for example, were influenced by the legendary Ferrari 308 GTB. In the 1980s one of these had appeared in the TV show *Magnum, PI*, and it became one of the most famous Ferraris ever built.

Where the 488 GTB really scored, though, was by being:

1 Super fast – for its engine size it is the most powerful road car Ferrari have ever made*

2 Easy to drive – the 488 GTB uses technology borrowed from Ferrari's Formula 1 cars, but computers tame the power so that ordinary drivers can cope with it.

What's it like to drive?

*The first time I find an empty bit of road and depress the throttle, it's apparent … that the 488's acceleration is a league beyond that of the 458, even beyond the **Lambo** Huracán, flinging you down the road with the shocking, brutal thrust of a fighter jet on take-off*

– Top Gear review, August 2015.

*Ferrari's F12 is the firm's most powerful car, but the 488 GTB produces more power per litre of engine size.

TOP SPEED

330 kph
(217 mph)

0–100 KPH

3.0 seconds

MAX POWER

492 kW
(660 bhp) @ 8,000 rpm

MAX TORQUE

760 Nm
(560 lb/ft) @ 3,000 rpm

THE 488 SPIDER

The 488 Spider is as powerful and beautiful as the GTB, but with one big difference. If you're driving and the sun comes out, just pull over, push a button and 14 seconds later the lightweight metal roof has folded itself away.

A Spider with the roof down is even more exciting to drive than the GTB. The engine and **exhaust** are easier to hear, and make a thrilling noise as you race up and down through the gears.

Double spoiler at front of car: increases **downforce** and engine cooling

Computer-controlled magnetic suspension adapts to road surface

NAME: Enzo Ferrari
LIVED: 1898–1988
FAMOUS AS: Founder of Ferrari

Between 1920 and 1931, Enzo was a racing driver for Alfa Romeo. He started his own car company in 1939, and its first car, the Ferrari 125 S, appeared in 1947. Just five years later, in 1952, a Ferrari driver won the FIA Formula One World Championship. In the next 55 years, Ferrari drivers went on to win the world title again 14 times – more than any other manufacturer.

Max RPM:
9,000

Engine:
3902 cc

Weight:
1,420 kg

Fuel use per 100 km:
11.4 litres

CO2:
260 g/km

Gearbox:
7-speed **dual-clutch** automatic

Drive:
rear wheels

Main body:
aluminium

Frame:
aluminium

Braking:
ceramic/carbon

FERRARI
F12 BERLINETTA

The F12 Berlinetta does not have turbochargers – it doesn't need them. To make it go fast (really fast), the F12 just has an absolutely enormous 6262 cc, **V12** engine.

Factory: Maranello, Italy

Most powerful Ferrari engine ever produced – 80 per cent of torque is produced at only 2,500 rpm

Scooped bonnet shape creates downforce

Many supercar fans do not like turbochargers. Turbochargers work by using the car's exhaust gas to drive a turbine. The turbine helps push extra oxygen into the engine **cylinders**. Oxygen is needed for fuel to burn: the extra oxygen allows more fuel to be burned. This produces more power. So far it all sounds like a good thing, but …

Turbochargers have two problems:
• the process causes a slight delay in acceleration, compared to a non-turbo engine*;
• they make a whizzing, whirring noise that many supercar fans absolutely HATE!

If you hate turbos, the F12 Berlinetta is probably one of your dream cars. Even without turbos, it is the second most-powerful and fastest car Ferrari makes.

Air vents to front brakes open when cooling is needed

Two clutches and a computer choose the gear for you

NAME: Flavio Manzoni
LIVED: 1965–present
FAMOUS AS: Architect and car designer

When the F12 Berlinetta won the 2014 **Compasso d'oro** design award, the prize was collected by Flavio Manzoni, who is in charge of design at Ferrari. As well as the F12, Manzoni worked on the 458 Italia and the LaFerrari (see page 10). Pre Ferrari he worked on cars as different as the Fiat 500 and Bugatti's supercars.

What's it like to drive?

You come across a long, dark tunnel. Windows down … pin the throttle and instantly you could be in Monaco in Grand Prix week. From the screaming exhausts as you're hurled through the darkness, to the loud crack as a gear change fires through and extinguishes the red LEDs on the top of the steering wheel, the F12 is pure race car.

– *Evo* review, June 2014

*Non-turbo engines are called 'normally aspirated' engines.

The steering wheel borrows technology from Ferrari's Formula 1 cars. Every control can be reached with your hands on the steering wheel.

TOP SPEED

340 kph
(211 mph)

0–100 KPH

3.1 seconds

MAX POWER

545 kW
(730 bhp) @ 8,250 rpm

MAX TORQUE

690 Nm
(509lb/ft) @ 6,000 rpm

 Max RPM:
8,700

 Engine:
6262 cc

 Weight:
1,525 kg

 Fuel use per 100 km:
15 litres

 CO2:
350 g/km

 Gearbox:
7-speed dual-clutch automatic

 Drive:
rear wheels

 Main body:
aluminium

 Frame:
aluminium

 Braking:
carbon-ceramic

Price Tag...

When it was released in 2013, the most basic F12 Berlinetta cost around £250,000 plus tax. That's a lot of pocket money. Adding extras like Ferrari's HELE system (a **stop-start system** that can restart the car in milliseconds) could take the price as high as £330,000.

F12 BERLINETTA TIMELINE

1987
F40 is released: the last Ferrari approved by the company's founder, Enzo, before his death. The F40 is the fastest, most powerful and most expensive Ferrari ever made.

2006
599 GTB appears: at the time, with 612 bhp, it is Ferrari's most powerful car

2013
F12 Berlinetta: faster, more powerful and lighter than the 599 GTB, it wins Car of the Year in several countries

FERRARI
LAFERRARI

Factory: Maranello, Italy

For fans of the Ferrari Formula 1 team, the LaFerrari has to be the ultimate car. It is crammed with technology from the factory's race cars. Ferrari say that this car has, "the most extreme performance ever".

Pedal controls for brake and accelerator can be adjusted to suit driver

The doors of LaFerrari swing upwards and are made of impact-resistant carbon fibre, the same material used in the nose cones of Ferrari's F1 cars.

Air flows out over bonnet, adding downforce

Air enters at front and out of bonnet for added downforce

La Ferrari is Italian for 'The Ferrari'. The name tells you that this is the car Ferrari is most proud of. It is the first car they have ever built that uses hybrid petrol-electric power. Not only does the LaFerrari have the most powerful engine Ferrari has ever made, a 6262 cc V12 engine, but it also has an electric motor that can add another 120 kW (160 bhp) of power.

ELECTRIC POWER

The LaFerrari's electric batteries are recharged every time the driver brakes. The system captures the force of the car slowing down, and stores it as electrical energy. This energy is then reused to power the electric motor whenever an extra boost of speed is needed. The technology is used in Ferrari Formula 1 cars – but the LaFerrari's system is even more complex.

Price Tag...

When it came out the LaFerrari cost a minimum of £900,000, before tax. In 2014 the first used LaFerrari came up for sale. It had been driven for 200 km, and the price was just over … £2 million. In 2016, Ferrari announced that the final, 500th car would be auctioned to help those affected by an earthquake in central Italy.

LAFERRARI TIMELINE

The 250 GTO, based on a race car, is released; in 2012 the GTO became the world's most expensive car when one was sold for just over £30 million

The Enzo, named after the firm's founder, is released. It combines Formula 1 technology with **driver aids** that are not allowed in Formula 1 at the time. Only 399 Enzos are ever built.

The F50 appears; it uses an engine developed from the 1990 Ferrari Formula 1 car

TOP SPEED
over **350** kph
(217 mph)

0–100 KPH
under **3** seconds

MAX POWER
708 kW
(950 bhp) @ 9,000 rpm

MAX TORQUE
900 Nm
(664lb/ft) @ 6,750 rpm

Air intakes on rear wheel arches help force air into the engine, increasing power by 3.5 kW

Indent behind front wheels increases downforce

Carbon fibre is baked at 130–150°C for ideal strength

Driver sits in reclined position, similar to that in a Formula 1 car

Max RPM:
9,250

Engine:
6262 cc V12 plus electric motor

Weight:
1,255 kg

Fuel use per 100 km:
not known

CO2:
330 g/km

Gearbox:
7-speed dual-clutch automatic

Drive:
rear wheels

Main body:
carbon fibre **tub** with Kevlar® protection

Frame:
aluminium

Braking:
carbon-ceramic

NAME: Rory Byrne
LIVED: 1944–present
FAMOUS AS: Formula 1 engineer and car designer

When Ferrari wanted to bring Formula 1 technology into the LaFerrari, they asked the legendary engineer Rory Byrne to help.

In the late 1990s and early 2000s, Ferrari was the most successful team in Formula 1. The team had a brilliant driver, Michael Schumacher – but they also had a brilliant engineer, Byrne. Between 1996, when he joined Ferrari, and 2004, Byrne's cars won 71 Formula 1 races, five Driver Championships for Schumacher, and six Constructor Championships for the firm.

LAMBORGHINI
CENTENARIO

Centenario is Italian for '100th birthday'. A hundred years after Ferruccio Lamborghini was born, the company he began released the Centenario. It is the ultimate Lambo.

Factory: Sant'Agata Bolognese, Italy

Lightweight carbon-fibre body

Computer controls can set engine and suspension in three different modes

What's it like to drive?

Goodness it's fast. The V12 engine gives you a real thump in the back with every gearshift, and it spears towards the horizon at a pace that only a few other cars on the planet can compete with.

– *What Car?* reviews the V12 engine used in the Centenario

Air intakes cool engine and brakes, and provide downforce

Price Tag...

The Centenario costs around £1.5 million – but even if your (giant) piggy bank is full, you are too late. Every one of the 40 Centenarios was sold before it had even been built.

The Centenario is a typical Lambo supercar – but with the volume turned up to 11. It has the most powerful engine Lamborghini has ever made. Every possible body panel is made of super-light carbon fibre. Even the frame is made of carbon fibre instead of metal. So ... what do you get when you add super-light to super-powerful?

SUPER FAST!

To understand just how fast, try this. Say, "One potato, two potato, three potato, four." By the time you got to the "three po ...", the Centenario would have been doing 100 kph.

(Even a Formula 1 car would only have got to that speed at "three ...".) After 23 "potatoes", the Centenario would have been doing over 300 kph.

CENTENARIO TIMELINE

1963 · 1973 · · · 2001 2010 2016 ·

Centenario

Aventador

Countach, the most famous supercar of the 1970s

Murciélago

350 GTV – the first Lamborghini

Carbon-fibre race seats

V12 engine behind seats

All four wheels get power

Spoiler creates downforce to rear wheels

Spoiler can be in three different positions depending on speed

TOP SPEED
350 kph
(217 mph)

0–100 KPH
2.8 seconds

MAX POWER
566 kW
(759 bhp) @ 8,500 rpm

MAX TORQUE
690 Nm
(507 lb/ft) @ 5,500 rpm

Max RPM:
8,600

Engine:
6498 cc

Weight:
1,520 kg

Fuel use per 100 km:
15.7 litres

CO2:
370 g/km

Gearbox:
7-speed dual-clutch automatic

Drive:
all wheels

Main body:
carbon fibre

Frame:
carbon fibre **monocoque**

Braking:
ceramic/carbon

NAME: Ferruccio Lamborghini
LIVED: 1916–93
FAMOUS AS: Founder of Lamborghini

Ferruccio Lamborghini was a successful Italian businessman whose company made tractors. He owned a Ferrari — but it kept breaking down. When Lamborghini complained to Enzo Ferrari, he was rudely told to, "go back to making tractors." Lamborghini decided to teach Ferrari a lesson by building a better car himself. By 1963, Lamborghini had designed his first supercar, the 350 GTV.

LAMBORGHINI
HURACÁN LP 610-4

Huracán is Italian for 'hurricane'. It is also the name of a famous fighting bull. Many Lamborghinis, from the Miura onwards, have been named after bulls.

Factory: Sant'Agata Bolognese, Italy

The Huracán is a very important car for Lamborghini. It replaced the Gallardo, the most popular Lamborghini ever made. Buyers loved the Gallardo's raw power and lack of technology (at least, compared to a McLaren or a Ferrari). Over 14,000 Gallardos were made and sold.

The Huracán uses a new version of the Gallardo's 5.2 litre V10 engine, and is more powerful. Even better, the driver feels 70 per cent of the engine's pull at just 1,000 rpm – fewer **revs** than you use to pull away from a parking space. The Huracán is more aerodynamic than the Gallardo, and has better brakes and suspension, and an improved gearbox. In fact, almost every part of the Huracán is an improvement on the most successful Lamborghini ever.

Today there are several different models of Huracán. They include an open-topped Spyder version and the LP 610-4 *Polizia* produced for the Italian police. To get away from one of those, you'd have to be a Formula 1 driver in another supercar!

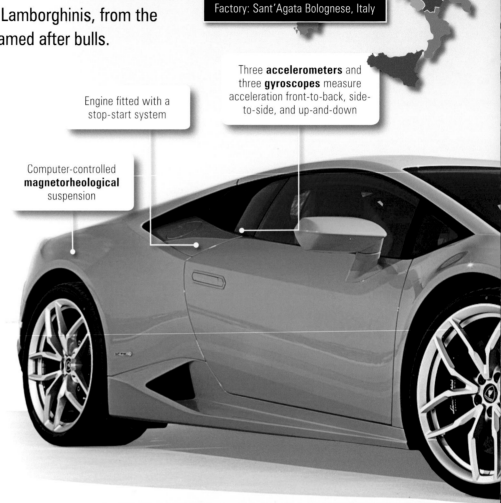

Engine fitted with a stop-start system

Three **accelerometers** and three **gyroscopes** measure acceleration front-to-back, side-to-side, and up-and-down

Computer-controlled **magnetorheological** suspension

HURACÁN TIMELINE

1981	2003	2014
The Jalpa, a 2-seater with a V8 engine, named after a famous breed of fighting bull	Gallardo (also named after a fighting bull) released. It is the company's first 'baby' V10 supercar.	The first Huracán (named after yet another famous bull) appears

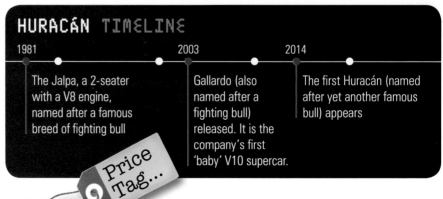

Price Tag...

The Huracán starts at about £180,000 before tax, but adding extras means that almost everyone pays more than that. Do not expect to save any money buying one that's been used, second-hand versions cost almost the same as a basic new one.

TOP SPEED

325 kph
(202 mph)

0–100 KPH

3.2 seconds

MAX POWER

449 kW
(602 bhp) @ 8,250 rpm

MAX TORQUE

560 Nm
(412 lb/ft) @ 6,500 rpm

ANIMA button on bottom spoke of steering wheel: changes settings from Strada (street) to Sport and Corsa (race), controlling throttle response, gear change, suspension, drive control, the intake and exhaust noise flaps, and more...

Paddles behind steering wheel allow driver to control gear changes

 Max RPM:
8,500

 Engine:
5204 cc V10

 Weight:
1,422 kg

 Fuel use per 100 km:
12.5 litres

 CO2:
280 g/km

 Gearbox:
7-speed dual-clutch automatic

 Drive:
all wheels

 Main body:
aluminium

 Frame:
aluminium and carbon

 Braking:
ceramic-carbon

What's it like to drive?

Amazing styling, shocking engine note, hopelessly impractical (the trunk will barely fit a backpack), hilarious fun on track, and some craziness that could only work on a Lambo, like the ... inability to see anything behind you. It just works, it's the wild essence of a Lamborghini.

– Jalopnik review

VENENO ROADSTER

The Roadster is based on the Veneno, which was built as a "racing prototype for the road". The Veneno's super-light body and massive aerodynamic features made it look like something out of a *Batman* movie.

Factory: Sant'Agata Bolognese, Italy

Lamborghini announced that "not more than nine" Veneno Roadsters were to be built. The Roadster (essentially a Veneno, but without a roof) is handmade from carbon fibre, which makes it extremely lightweight.

Everything, from the engine to the seats and wheels, has been made as high performance and high quality as possible.

Body panels and dashboard are all carbon fibre

Carbon fibre is widely used so that the Roadster is super-lightweight.

Central tunnel is part of the car's monocoque frame

NAME:	Valentino Balboni
LIVED:	1948–present
FAMOUS AS:	Lamborghini test/development driver

Lightweight seats are carbon fibre

Balboni had a car fan's idea of a dream job: Lamborghini test driver. (Imagine coming home and telling your mum that!) He started working at Lamborghini as an apprentice mechanic when he was 19, in 1968, just a few years after the company had started. As test driver he drove Lamborghinis thousands of kilometres a year, spotting problems and suggesting possible improvements.

After Balboni retired in 2008, the company released the Lamborghini Gallardo LP550-2 Valentino Balboni, named in his honour.

Aero ducts (top) and air intakes channel air to provide downforce

VENENO ROADSTER TIMELINE

1995 — Lamborghini releases the Diablo Roadster: unlike the Veneno Roadster, the Diablo had a removable **targa top**

2004 — The Lamborghini Murciélago Roadster: an open-cockpit version of the famous V12 Murciélago supercar

2014 — The Veneno Roadster is released

(221 mph)

0–100 KPH
2.9 seconds

MAX POWER
552 kW
(740 bhp) @ 8,400 rpm

MAX TORQUE
690 Nm
(507 lb/ft) @ 5,500 rpm

Side air ducts channel air to rear to improve aerodynamics

Angle of rear wing adjusts to suit speed and road type

Roll bar behind seats protects passengers in a crash

Wheels are designed to channel air onto the brakes, cooling them down

Max RPM:
8,400

Engine:
6498 cc V12

Weight:
1,490 kg

Fuel use per 100 km:
6 litres

CO2:
370 g/km

Gearbox:
7-speed dual-clutch automatic

Drive:
all wheels

Main body:
carbon fibre

Frame:
carbon fibre

Braking:
carbon-ceramic

Price Tag...

At just about £3.6 million, depending on local taxes, a new Veneno Roadster was the world's most expensive car. These days if you want one you'd have to try and find it used. Start saving your Christmas money, though, because in 2016 a Veneno that had travelled 800 km was offered for sale at £9 million.

GRANTURISMO MC STRADALE

Maserati was founded by the Maserati brothers in 1914. The five brothers set out to build the best, fastest race cars in the world. Their company has been making high-performance cars ever since.

GRANTURISMO MC STRADALE TIMELINE

1992 · **1998** · **2010**

Maserati releases the 3200 GT, a 3.2 L V8

The first MC Stradale cars are produced

The Ghibli GT, a 2.0 L (in Italy) or 2.8 L (everywhere else) twin-turbo engine. In 1996 one of these 'Biturbo' engines was used in a speedboat that broke the world water-speed record.

Factory: Modena, Italy

Carbon fibre seats and bonnet reduce weight

Rear is shaped to help draw air from under the car, adding speed

Like most supercars, the GranTurismo MC Stradale has a **splitter**. This part at the front of a car splits the air the car is going through.

Above the splitter the air is slowed down

Pressure above the splitter presses down, adding grip for the front wheels

Below the splitter air flows freely

NAME: Battista Farina
LIVED: 1893–1966
FAMOUS AS: Car designer

Farina's nickname was "Pinin". He started working in a garage when he was 11, and when he opened his own car-design workshop he called it Carrozzeria Pininfarina. Pininfarina soon became one of the most famous car-design workshops in Italy. Since then, the company has designed cars for Maserati, Ferrari, Alfa Romeo and many others. Farina himself made many of the designs; later, the company was run by his son, then his grandson.

TOP SPEED
303 kph
(188 mph)

0–100 KPH
4.5 seconds

MAX POWER
343 kW
(460 bhp) @ 7,000 rpm

MAX TORQUE
520 Nm
(383 lb/ft) @ 4,750 rpm

MOTOR-RACING HISTORY

Maserati race cars have been driven to victory in many Grands Prix in Europe. They have also won the **Indy 500** twice. Today, though, Maserati no longer makes race cars. The company produces high-performance road cars – and the highest performance of all is the GranTurismo MC Stradale.

The MC Stradale is a grand tourer, or GT. This kind of car is designed to be driven long distances and still be comfortable. GT cars are also raced all around the world, in North America, Europe and Asia-Pacific. The most famous GT races are in the World Endurance Championship. Maserati produces a track-racing version of the GranTurismo MC, called the GT4.

Three driver settings: normal auto, sport **manual** and race manual

In race mode the gear change takes 0.06 seconds

Front splitter, bonnet slit and air ducts aid aerodynamics and cooling

 Max RPM:
7,200

 Engine:
4691 cc V8

 Weight:
1,700 kg

 Fuel use per 100 km:
15.5 litres

 CO2:
360 g/km

 Gearbox:
6-speed automatic

 Drive:
rear wheels

 Main body:
aluminium

Frame:
aluminium

Braking:
carbon-ceramic

What's it like to drive?

*I don't get the sense that the machine is doing all the hard work for me (although it probably is) … I'm fighting against the onslaught on **understeer**, balancing the car against roll in the turns, trying to find the sweet spot for the next gear change… And it feels … right.*

– crankandpiston.com review

PAGANI
HUAYRA BC

Once described as 'Satan's pet catfish' because of its crazy-looking mirror stalks, the Huayra was named after a South American wind god. When this car blows past you at 360 kph, you understand why! When it first appeared in 2012, the Huayra was an instant success.

Despite costing around £1 million, the original Huayra sold out by the end of 2015. Pagani could not make any more, because they had only been able to buy 100 engines from their engine builder, Mercedes-AMG. Then, in 2016, came the news that Pagani was building a new, even more extreme version: the Huayra BC. (The 'BC' is in honour of Benny Caiola, the first person who ever bought a Pagani car, back in 1992.)

The Huayra BC is a stripped-out, stripped-down speed machine. The engine is more powerful than before and the car is lighter. Every body panel except the roof has been re-shaped to increase speed and grip.

What's it like to drive?

The steering is sharper ... the brakes are mighty, and the performance is brutal ... delivering the kind of acceleration you can feel in your face.

– *topgear.com* review, February 2016

Stalk-mounted side mirrors add to the Huayra's catfish appearance

Huge, adjustable rear wing adds downforce

Huayra BC uses a new type of carbon fibre, and is 132 kg lighter than the original car

Manual gearbox is 40 per cent lighter than an automatic one

Engine mounted right behind driver makes this a noisy car!

Air that has cooled the brakes leaves through these ducts

The Zonda, made mostly of carbon fibre, is released

Pagani Automobili Modena is founded

The Huayra BC is announced

The Huayra, another mainly carbon fibre car, is released

(224 mph)

0–100 KPH

3 seconds

MAX POWER

552 kW

(750 bhp) @ 6,200 rpm

MAX TORQUE

1000 Nm

(738 lb/ft) @ 4,000 rpm

NAME: Horacio Pagani
LIVED: 1955–present
FAMOUS AS: Founder of Pagani

Pagani is Argentinian, but his family originally came from Italy. As a boy he built models of his fantasy cars out of balsa wood, and dreamed of one day building his own supercar. By the time he was 20, Pagani had already designed and built a **Formula 3** race car.

In 1983, Pagani moved to Italy. He worked for Lamborghini, on their Countach Evoluzione. This was an early experiment in carbon fibre supercars. After Lamborghini decided not to continue with carbon-fibre, Pagani left. In 1992 he started his own supercar company.

Price Tag...

You might want one, but you can't – even if you have got the £2 million asking price. Only 20 BCs will ever be made, and all were sold before the car was available. Almost every Huayra BC Roadster (an open-topped version) is also pre-sold, despite the fact that when they ordered them the buyers had not even seen what it looked like.

Max RPM:

6,500

Engine:

5980 cc V12 twin turbo

Weight:

1,218 kg

Fuel use per 100 km:

20 litres

CO2:

131 g/km

Gearbox:

7-speed manual single-clutch

Drive:

rear wheels

Main body:

carbon fibre

Frame:

carbon fibre/ titanium monocoque

Braking:

carbon-ceramic

Air exits over the bonnet, providing downforce

Body panels re-shaped to increase downforce and lessen **drag**

Air is channelled into the new front splitter, improving aerodynamics and cooling

ZONDA REVOLUCION

> When the Zonda design first appeared in 1999, it was an instant hit. Ever since, Pagani has been developing lighter, more powerful, faster versions of the car. The Revolucion is the ultimate Zonda.

Factory: San Cesario sul Panaro, Italy

RACE CAR PERFORMANCE

The Revolucion is designed to be used only on a race track, and weighs just over a tonne – that's 70 per cent as much as a Ferrari F12. Plus, with more power, the Revolucion is half a second faster than the F12 to 100 kph.

Many of the Revolucion's features have been borrowed from the world's top race cars. Like a Formula 1 car, the Revolucion has aerodynamics that can be adjusted for maximum top speed or for maximum downforce. The rear wing has a **DRS** system inspired by Formula 1 technology. DRS changes the angle of the wing, allowing it to slip through the air more quickly if rear grip is not needed.

The trouble is that the Zonda Revolucion is so noisy, in many countries it breaks the noise limit even for race tracks, and it's certainly not allowed on public roads. About the only place you can drive it is on a private racetrack in the middle of nowhere.

Steel roll cage

Overall weight is less than a Mini Cooper

HANS-based carbon-fibre seats

What's it like to drive?

Simply sensational, pulling relentlessly with a soundtrack straight from Le Mans.

– *autocar.co.uk* review

Price Tag...

The Zonda Revolucion is priced at around £2 million plus tax. Pagani still lists the car (and nine other Zonda models) on its website, but all have apparently now been sold.

The Revolucion's rear wing is part of its Formula 1 style aerodynamics and braking systems.

With the wing 'open' (parallel with the ground), the car is more aerodynamic

With the wing 'closed' (at an angle to the ground), the car has more grip

Gear shifts controlled using paddles behind steering wheel

TOP SPEED
over **350** kph
(217 mph)

0–100 KPH
2.6 seconds

MAX POWER
588 kW
(788 bhp) @ 8,000 rpm

MAX TORQUE
730 Nm
(538 lb/ft) @ 5,800 rpm

Magnesium gearbox shifts in 0.02 seconds

Traction control system has 12 different settings

Anti-lock brake system stops the car skidding while slowing down

Max RPM:
est. **8,000**

Engine:
5987 cc V12

Weight:
1,070 kg

Fuel use per 100 km:
est. **20 litres**

CO2:
est. **500 g/km**

Gearbox:
6-speed automatic

Drive:
rear wheels

Main body:
carbon fibre

Frame:
carbon-titanium blend

Braking:
carbon-ceramic

ZONDA REVOLUCION TIMELINE

1999 2007 2013

The first Zonda, the C12, appears. Only five were ever built – and one was used for crash testing!

The Zonda Revolucion is revealed

The Zonda R, a track version of the road car, appears. Although the R looks like the road car, it is said to use only 10 per cent of the same parts.

ALFA ROMEO
4C

The 4C is the Italian supercar ordinary people might just be able to afford. It costs so little (compared to a Pagani or a Lamborghini, anyway) that Alfa calls it a 'junior supercar'.

Factory: Modena, Italy

The 4C is the small car with the heart of a race star – almost everyone who has driven a 4C says that, while it might have its faults, it is absolutely great. One reviewer even said: "Give me a [race] track to play on, and I'd choose a 4C over any Ferrari."

Engine produces 80 per cent of its power at just 1,700 rpm – just as it is pulling away

What is the 4C's secret? The main reasons it is so popular are:

1 It's light
Heavy cars need a lot of power to go fast. When they designed the 4C, the engineers knew they wanted it to be light. This meant a less powerful engine could be fitted.

The glass is 10 per cent thinner than on a normal car, saving about 15 per cent weight

2 It's cheap
The 4C costs the same as one-third of a Lamborghini Huracán. For the same price as a used LaFerrari (see page 10), you could buy 35 Alfa Romeo 4Cs.

Body panels made of SMC, a form of fibreglass that is lighter than aluminium

3 It's not like anything else
Every other supercar is loaded with electronic driver aids, but the 4C has very few. Many drivers enjoy this. It makes them feel that they are in charge, rather than the car's computers.

Disc brakes on all four wheels: the 4C can go from 100 kph to 0 in 36 m

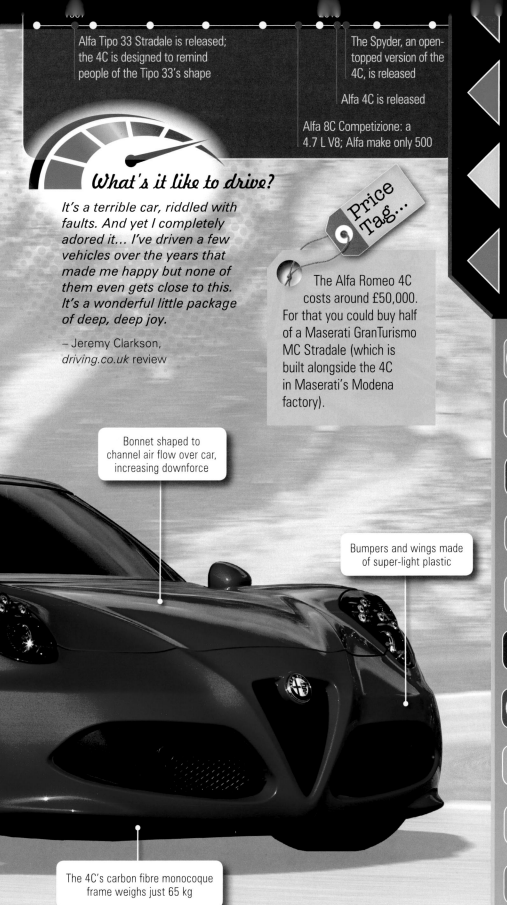

Alfa Tipo 33 Stradale is released; the 4C is designed to remind people of the Tipo 33's shape

The Spyder, an open-topped version of the 4C, is released

Alfa 4C is released

Alfa 8C Competizione: a 4.7 L V8; Alfa make only 500

2⌀⌀ kph
(160 mph)

0–100 KPH
4.5 seconds

MAX POWER
177 kW
(237 bhp) @ 6,000 rpm

MAX TORQUE
350 Nm
(258 lb/ft) @ 2,200 rpm

What's it like to drive?

It's a terrible car, riddled with faults. And yet I completely adored it… I've driven a few vehicles over the years that made me happy but none of them even gets close to this. It's a wonderful little package of deep, deep joy.

– Jeremy Clarkson,
driving.co.uk review

Price Tag…

The Alfa Romeo 4C costs around £50,000. For that you could buy half of a Maserati GranTurismo MC Stradale (which is built alongside the 4C in Maserati's Modena factory).

Bonnet shaped to channel air flow over car, increasing downforce

Bumpers and wings made of super-light plastic

The 4C's carbon fibre monocoque frame weighs just 65 kg

Max RPM:
6,500

Engine:
1742 CC turbo charged **inline 4**

Weight:
895 kg

Fuel use per 100 km:
6.9 litres

CO2:
157 g/km

Gearbox:
6-speed twin clutch automatic

Drive:
rear wheels

Main body:
lightweight fibreglass **composite**

Frame:
carbon fibre monocoque

Braking:
lightweight alloy/steel discs

THE ITALIAN SUPERCAR FROM... FRANCE?

BUGATTI

Bugatti is a French supercar maker, owned by Volkswagen (from Germany). But Bugatti was founded by an Italian – which is the excuse for including it in a book about Italian supercars.

Factory: Molsheim, France

THE WORLD'S FASTEST CAR

Today, Bugatti is famous for making the world's fastest car, the Veyron. When the Veyron was first released in 2005, it took the supercar world by storm. Then in 2010 a new, even faster version of the Veyron appeared: the Super Sport. In 2013 a Super Sport broke the world record for the world's fastest production car, with 431 kph (268 mph).

THE NEXT WORLD'S FASTEST CAR?

In late 2016, Bugatti's new supercar, the Chiron (right), was released. With 300 bhp more power than a Veyron, it is believed that without a speed limiter, it could reach over 463 kph (280 mph). Named after racing driver Louis Chiron, the Chiron has increased performance by 25 per cent compared to the Veyron, largely as a result of a complete engine and turbocharger re-design.

Central fin from the top of the grille provides stability

NACA ducts on roof circulate air to engine

900 l of water a minute are pumped through the radiator to help cool the engine

Tyres specially designed with Michelin

Price Tag...

The Bugatti Chiron costs around £2.2 million plus taxes, and has been limited to a product run of just 500. Current Bugatti owners are believed to be preferred customers, with one wealthy owner buying six Chirons!

What's it like to drive?

You put your foot down and feel your internal organs [being] squeezed to one side under the sheer g-force ... it can throw you at the horizon with sufficient force to make you feel physically uncomfortable.

– Veyron review by *autocar.co.uk*

The 16.4 Super Sport
is released

The Chiron is
released

The Veyron Grand Sport, a targa
top version, comes out

Veyron 16.4 is released (its name comes from having
16 cylinders with four valves in each)

420 kph
(268 mph) (limited)

0–100 KPH
2.5 seconds

MAX POWER
1103 kW
(1479 bhp) @ 2,000 rpm

MAX TORQUE
1600 Nm
(1180 lb/ft) @ 2,000 rpm

Rear tyre is the widest ever
fitted to a production car; four
new tyres cost over £40,000

Max RPM:
7,000

Engine:
7993 cc quad turbo W16

Weight:
1,995 kg

Fuel use per 100 km:
not available

CO_2:
not available

Gearbox:
7-speed twin clutch
automatic

Drive:
all wheels

Main body:
carbon fibre

Frame:
carbon fibre/steel/aluminium
monocoque

Braking:
carbon-silicon carbide

The Chiron's spoiler doubles
as an air brake as part of the
car's active aerodynamics

NAME: Ettore Bugatti
LIVED: 1881–1947
FAMOUS AS: Founder of Bugatti

Ettore Bugatti was born in Milan, Italy in 1881. While still a teenager he
designed and built his first cars. Bugatti's work was seen by the nobleman
Baron de Dietrich, who owned a car factory in Germany. He asked Bugatti
to come and design cars for him.

By 1909, Bugatti had set up his own factory, in Molsheim*. The company
became famous for its racing cars: a Bugatti won the first ever Monaco Grand
Prix, in 1929. In fact, six of the top seven finishers were driving Bugattis.

*From 1871–1918 Molsheim was part of Germany (and again during the Second World War, from 1940–44).

The supercars in this book are the fastest, newest and most technologically advanced supercars made in Italy. But lots of other famous Italian supercars have been manufactured since 2000. Here are a few of them:

MANUFACTURER: FERRARI
MODEL: F60 ENZO
YEAR: 2002

When the F60 Enzo came out, it looked like a **gull-winged** vision of the future. Today, it still looks like a gull-winged vision of the future. This was the first Ferrari production car to be built around a carbon fibre tub.

MANUFACTURER: FERRARI
MODEL: F430
YEAR: 2004

Said to be the biggest-selling Ferrari of all time, the F430 road car also came in a Spider convertible version (shown) and a lighter, more powerful Scuderia version. Ferrari also made a track version, the GTC.

MANUFACTURER: MAZZANTI
MODEL: MILLECAVALLI
YEAR: 2016

An extreme version of a car that's already pretty extreme, the Mazzanti Evantra. The Millecavalli's 7.2 l twin-turbo engine rockets it to 100 kph in a scorching 2.8 seconds. And if you can find a long enough bit of road, this lightweight supercar will quickly hit over 400 kph.

MANUFACTURER: LAMBORGHINI
MODEL: GALLARDO
YEAR: 2003

The Gallardo was fitted with a 5 L V10 engine, and was replaced by the Huracán. Two Italian police Gallardos, used mainly to carry transplant organs, are said to have been "destroyed in the line of duty".

MANUFACTURER: LAMBORGHINI
MODEL: MURCIELAGO
YEAR: 2001

The Murcielago is the car that came before the Aventador. It had the typical features of a modern Lamborghini: sharp edges, a powerful V12 engine and a huge price tag. The Murcielago was named after a legendary bull, which in 1879 survived a battle with a famous matador. The bull retired, and fathered the famous breed of fighting bulls called Miura (see pages 4–5).

MANUFACTURER: LAMBORGHINI
MODEL: AVENTADOR
YEAR: 2011

The car the even-more-expensive Centenario and Veneno Roadster are based on, the Aventador is loved by celebrities everywhere. Famous owners include Kanyé West, Justin Bieber and Cristiano Ronaldo.

MANUFACTURER: MASERATI
MODEL: MC12
YEAR: 2004

Maserati only made this car so that they could enter a racing version in the GT Racing Championship. It was based on a Ferrari Enzo's engine and frame. Twenty-five road versions were made: owners got a 6.0 L V12 engine that shot the car to 100 kph in just 3.8 seconds.

MANUFACTURER: ALFA ROMEO
MODEL: 8C
YEAR: 2007

Based on the Maserati GranTurismo, but looking completely different, the 8C is consistently voted one of the most beautiful cars Alfa has ever made. A 444 bhp V8 engine and 0–100 kph time of 4.2 seconds help it along.

Italian car companies have been making supercars for longer than anyone else. From companies such as Lamborghini, which still makes supercars today, to firms like Lancia, here are just a few of the most famous oldies:

MANUFACTURER: FERRARI
MODEL: 166 MM BARCHETTA
YEAR: 1948

One of the most beautiful Ferraris ever built, only 25 166s were ever made. It came first and second in the famous **Mille Miglia** race in 1949. The car that finished second was sold in 2013 for around £2.5 million.

MANUFACTURER: FERRARI
MODEL: 330 P4 BERLINETTA
YEAR: 1967

In 1966, Ford GT40s won the top three places at the Le Mans 24 Hour Endurance Race. The 330 P4 is the car Ferrari built in response. In 1967 it won the 24 Hours of Daytona in Ford's backyard … but could only manage second at Le Mans, behind a GT40.

MANUFACTURER: LAMBORGHINI
MODEL: URRACO
YEAR: 1973

The Urraco is one of the cars that set Lamborghini's modern design style – despite coming out in 1972. The hard edges and straight lines would later become even more noticeable in the Countach (see below). The Urraco's V8 engine could hit 100 kph in fewer than 6 seconds.

MANUFACTURER: LAMBORGHINI
MODEL: COUNTACH
YEAR: 1974

In the 1970s and 1980s, every car-loving kid in the world knew all about the Countach. Designed by the legendary car designer Marcello Gandini, the Countach was so popular with buyers that Lamborghini only stopped making the car in 1990.

MANUFACTURER: LANCIA
MODEL: D24 SPIDER
YEAR: 1953

One of the greatest Lancias, the D24 car won the 1953 **Carrera Panamericana**, the 1954 Mille Miglia and the 1954 **Targa Florio**.

MANUFACTURER: MASERATI
MODEL: BORA
YEAR: 1971

The Bora was Maserati's fightback against the Lamborghini Miura. It was the first Maserati with the engine placed in the middle of the car – a big tick on the supercar checklist. For a supercar, the Bora was practical and comfortable: every wheel had its own separate suspension system and it even had luggage space under the bonnet!

PLACES TO VISIT

NATIONAL MOTOR MUSEUM
John Montagu Building
Beaulieu
Brockenhurst
Hampshire
SO42 7ZN

http://nationalmotormuseum.org.uk/
Supercars
Not a specialist supercar museum,
and focusing mainly on British cars,
the National Motor Museum is still
a great place for car fans to visit.
Its website has details of special
displays, which sometimes include
supercars.

BRITISH MOTOR MUSEUM
Banbury Road
Gaydon
Warwickshire
CV35 0BJ

https://www.britishmotormuseum.
co.uk
Like the National Motor Museum,
many of the cars are British, but other
countries' cars are also on display.

HAYNES MOTOR MUSEUM
Haynes International Motor Museum
Sparkford
Yeovil
Somerset
BA22 7LH

http://www.haynesmotormuseum.
com
With one collection known as 'Supercar
Century' and another titled 'Ferrari: The
Man, The Machine, The Myth', this is a
must-visit if you are nearby.

ITALY

MUSEO FERRARI
Via Dino Ferrari 43
41053 Maranello (MO)

http://museomaranello.ferrari.com
The museum's centrepiece is a
Formula 1 exhibition, complete
with cars and a pit-stop wall. There
are five other halls with different
exhibitions.

MUSEO ENZO FERRARI
via Paolo Ferrari 85
Modena

http://museomodena.ferrari.com
The museum is about Enzo Ferrari
and the cars he built or made
possible. It is the best place in the
world to find out what makes Ferrari
the supercar maker it is today.

MUSEO LAMBORGHINI
Automobili Lamborghini S.p.A.
Via Modena, 12
I-40019 Sant'Agata Bolognese (BO)

http://www.lamborghini.com/en/
museum/overview/
Here you can see just about every
supercar Lamborghini has ever
built. Highlights include the Miura,
Countach, Jalpa and other historical
models, plus Lamborghini's current
supercars.

PANINI MOTOR MUSEUM
Via Corletto Sud, 320
41126 MODENA

http://www.paninimotormuseum.it
This is really a Maserati museum.
It was named after the man who
prevented the original collection of
19 vintage Maseratis from being
sold, and instead made sure they
stayed in Modena, Italy. Since then
the collection has grown and it now
includes more recent Maseratis.

Please note: every effort has been made by the Publishers to
ensure that the websites in this book contain no inappropriate
or offensive material. However, because of the nature of the
Internet, it is impossible to guarantee that the contents of these
sites will not be altered. We strongly advise that Internet access
is supervised by a responsible adult.

accelerometer device that measures changes in speed

Carrera Panamericana long-distance motor race from the south of Mexico to the north; many people felt that the difficult driving conditions made it the world's most dangerous race

Compasso d'oro Italian for 'golden compass', the name of Italy's oldest and most respected industrial design award

composite made of a combination of different substances

cylinder space inside an engine where fuel is exploded, which pushes a piston down. The moving piston gives the car its power

downforce downward pressure on the tyres, which makes them grip the road better

drag air resistance

drive system providing power to the wheels, for example rear-wheel drive, front-wheel drive and all-wheel drive

driver aids technological features, such as traction control used to help the tyres grip the road surface, that help the driver

DRS short for Drag Reduction System, a way of adjusting the angle of a car's rear wing to make it more aerodynamic

dual-clutch gear-change system with two clutches: this allows a computer to pre-select the next gear, so that the car never loses power

exhaust to do with the waste material produced by an engine

Formula 3 racing category usually seen as the first serious step towards getting into Formula 1

GTB Gran Turismo Berlinetta

gull-winged Having doors that open up vertically, like flapping seagull wings

gyroscope device that measures changes in direction

Indy 500 short for 'Indianapolis 500', arguably the most famous motor race in North America

inline 4 engine with 4 cylinders set out in a straight line

Lambo short for Lamborghini

magnetorheological using fluid that changes how thick it is according to how much electricity is passed through it

manual gears that are changed by the driver, instead of being changed automatically

mid-mounted describes an engine that is behind the driver and passenger seats, where its weight helps all four wheels grip the road

Mille Miglia translated as 'thousand miles', the Mille Miglia is a famous Italian race held on public roads between 1927 and 1957

monocoque object that gets its strength from its outer layer, instead of a supporting frame or skeleton

NACA duct low-drag duct for air to pass into, originally designed by the US National Advisory Committee for Aeronautics (NACA) in 1945

production car car designed to be sold to the public and driven on ordinary roads

revs short for 'revolutions per minute' (rpm), a measure of how fast the engine is working

roll bar strong bar running up the sides and across the top of a car, to prevent driver/passengers being crushed if the car turns upside down in a crash

splitter aerodynamic blade or wing used to 'split' air as the car moves through it, usually to enhance downforce

stop-start system computer-controlled system for stopping a car's engine when it is not moving, then restarting it again when the driver wants to move off. Stop-start systems are a way of saving fuel and causing less pollution

Targa Florio motor race held in the mountains of Sicily between 1907 and 1977

targa top hard car roof that can be removed, turning the car into an open-top car

torque the amount of 'work' exerted by an engine

traction control system for adjusting power and braking so that a car does not skid

tub wide, long shape with raised sides and ends, and an open top

understeer turning less around a bend than the driver expected, considering how much he or she had turned the steering wheel

V12 engines are usually described using a combination of letters and numbers. A V12, for example, has 12 cylinders. They are arranged in two rows, joined at the bottom so that they make a V shape when seen from in front